Teen Communication Skills Workbook

Facilitator Reproducible Self-Assessments, Exercises & Educational Handouts

Ester A. Leutenberg
John J. Liptak, EdD

Illustrated by
Amy L. Brodsky, LISW-S

wholeperson
Stress & Wellness Publishers
Duluth, Minnesota

Whole Person
210 West Michigan Street
Duluth, MN 55802-1908

800-247-6789

books@wholeperson.com
www.wholeperson.com

Teen Communication Skills Workbook
Facilitator Reproducible Self-Assessments,
Exercises & Educational Handouts

Printed in the United States of America

10 9 8 7 6 5 4 3 2

Editorial Director: Carlene Sippola
Art Director: Joy Morgan Dey

Library of Congress Control Number:2012950495
ISBN: 978-1-57025-266-2

Using This Book *(For the professional)*

Interpersonal communication is the process of sending and receiving messages with another person. It sounds easy, but it is not. For teens, communicating effectively can be a very difficult process. The reason is that successful communication involves a very complex set of skills, as complex as those necessary for driving a car or reading a map. Part of the reason for this complexity is that messages can be communicated and received in a variety of ways, i.e. listening, speaking, signing, touch, eye contact. Teens need adequate communication skills in order to survive and thrive in our challenging society. Effective communication skills are critical in many walks of life including:

- Developing and maintaining friendships
- Participating in the community
- Doing well in school
- Functioning successfully in a group or family
- Maintaining and succeeding on a job
- Relating well with siblings
- Maintaining close relationships

Teens these days do not have adequate practice at communicating with others because of the use of texting, social networking, email and instant messaging. Teens rely on impersonal communication means and often lack the skills to engage in face-to-face communication. They may also lack an ability to read verbal and non-verbal cues and to understand tone.

The better the communication skills, the more prepared and successful teens will be. The good news is that communication skills can be taught, learned and improved through practice. Most teens typically learn their communication skills from their family, teachers and friends and thus bad communication habits arise when these people are poor role models. When teens do not have good communication skills, it is important for them to identify their areas of needed improvement and areas for growth, learn better ways of communicating with other people, and find ways to practice critical positive skills.

Over the last century, many different workbooks, workshops, and self-help systems have been designed to help people explore communication issues and blocks to skillful communication. In the past twenty years, many research studies have focused on the value of self-reflection and journaling as a way of exploring personal characteristics, identifying weak behaviors, and examining thoughts and feelings that lead to ineffective behaviors. This book is unique because it combines both powerful psychological tools designed to enhance communication skills: self-assessment and journaling.

The *Teen Communication Skills Workbook* contains five separate sections. In each, participants will learn more about themselves as well as the impact of skillful and non-skillful communicating:

- **Active Listening Scale** helps individuals determine how well they listen when communicating.
- **Nonverbal Communications Scale** helps individuals examine how their body language is affecting their interpersonal communications.
- **Communications Skills Scale** helps individuals measure how accomplished they are at using communication skills to initiate, build and maintain interpersonal relationships.
- **Cross-Cultural Communication Scale** helps individuals explore how well they communicate with people who are culturally different.
- **Negotiation Skills Scale** helps individuals explore how well they negotiate to get what they want without manipulating or alienating other people.

(Continued on the next page)

Using This Book *(For the professional, continued)*

These sections serve as avenues for individual self-reflection, as well as group experiences revolving around identified topics of importance. Each assessment includes directions for easy administration, scoring and interpretation. In addition, each section includes exploratory activities, reflective journaling activities and educational handouts to help participants discover their habitual, ineffective methods of communicating with others and to explore new ways for enhancing interpersonal communication.

By combining reflective assessment and journaling, participants will be exposed to a powerful method of communicating. Teens will become more aware of their strengths and areas needing improvement in using these skills.

Preparation for using the assessments and activities in this book is important. The authors suggest that prior to administering any of the assessments in this book, you complete them yourself. This will familiarize you with the format of the assessments, the scoring directions, the interpretation guides and the journaling activities. Although the assessments are designed to be self-administered, scored and interpreted, this familiarity will help prepare facilitators to answer questions about the assessments for participants.

Use Codes for Confidentiality

Confidentiality is a term for any action that preserves the privacy of other people. Because teens completing the activities in this workbook might be asked to answer assessment items and to journal about and explore their relationships, you will need to discuss confidentiality before you begin using the materials in this workbook. Maintaining confidentiality is important as it shows respect for others and allows participants to explore their feelings without hurting anyone's feelings or fearing gossip, harm or retribution.

In order to maintain confidentiality, explain to the participants that they need to assign a name code for each person they write about as they complete the various activities in the workbook. For example, a friend who they like named Debbie might be titled ILD (I Like Debbie) for a particular exercise. In order to protect their friends' identities, they cannot use people's actual names or initials, just codes.

The Assessments, Journaling Activities and Educational Handouts

The Assessments, Journaling Activities, and Educational Handouts in the *Teen Communication Skills Workbook* are reproducible and ready to be photocopied for participants' use. Assessments contained in this book focus on self-reported data and can be used by psychologists, counselors, teachers, therapists and career consultants. Accuracy and usefulness of the information provided is dependent on the truthful information that each participant provides through self-examination. By being honest, participants help themselves to learn about unproductive and ineffective patterns, and to uncover information that might be keeping them from being as happy and as successful as they might be.

An assessment instrument can provide participants with valuable information about themselves; however, it cannot measure or identify everything about them. The purpose of an assessment is not to pigeon-hole certain characteristics, but rather to allow participants to explore all of their characteristics. This book contains self-assessments, not tests. Tests measure knowledge or whether something is right or wrong. For the assessments in this book, there are no right or wrong answers. These assessments ask for personal opinions or attitudes about a topic of importance in the participant's life.

When administering assessments in this workbook, remember that the items are generically written so that they will be applicable to a wide variety of people but will not account for every possible variable for every person. Use them to help participants identify possible negative themes in their lives and find ways to break the hold that these patterns and their effects have.

Advise the participants taking the assessments that they should not spend too much time trying to analyze the content of the questions; their initial response will most likely be true. Regardless of individual scores, encourage participants to talk about their findings and their feelings pertaining to what they have discovered about themselves. Talking about listening, non-verbal communication, cross cultural relationships and negotiations skills can help teens in every aspect of their lives. These wellness exercises can be used by group facilitators working with any population who want to strengthen their overall wellness.

A particular score on any assessment does not guarantee a participant's level of communication skills. Use discretion when using any of the information or feedback provided in this workbook. The use of these assessments should not be substituted for consultation and/or wellness planning with a health care professional.

Thanks to the following professionals whose input into this book has been so valuable!

Carol Butler, MS Ed, RN, C
Annette Damien, MS, PPS
Beth Jennings, CTEC Counselor
Hannah Lavoie
Jay L. Leutenberg
Kathy Liptak, Ed.D.
Eileen Regen, M.Ed., CJE

Special thanks to Bill Hannes who reminds us that within diversities, people with physical disabilities as well as mental health issues are capable, bright and wise in many ways. We just need to take time to be aware of what they offer.

Layout of the Book

The *Teen Communication Skills Workbook* is designed to be used either independently or as part of an integrated curriculum. You may administer one of the assessments and the journaling exercises to an individual or a group with whom you are working, or you may administer a number of the assessments over one or more days.

This Book Includes the Following Reproducible Pages in the Five Sections:

- **Assessment Instruments** – Self-assessment inventories with scoring directions and interpretation materials. Group facilitators can choose one or more of the activities relevant to their participants.

- **Activity Handouts** – Practical questions and activities that prompt self-reflection and promote self-understanding. These questions and activities foster introspection and promote pro-social behaviors.

- **Quotations** – Quotations are used in each section to provide insight and promote reflection. Participants will be asked to select one or more of the quotations and journal about what the quotations mean to them.

- **Reflective Questions for Journaling** – Self-exploration activities and journaling exercises specific to each assessment to enhance self-discovery, learning, and healing.

- **Educational Handouts** – Handouts designed to enhance instruction can be used individually or in groups to promote a positive responsibility for communication at home, in the classroom, and in the community. They can be distributed, scanned and converted into masters for overheads or transparencies, projected or written on boards and/or discussed.

Who Should Use This Program?

This book has been designed as a practical tool for helping professionals, such as therapists, psychologists, guidance counselors, teachers, group leaders, etc. Depending on the role of the professional using the *Teen Communication Skills Workbook* and the specific group's needs, these sections can be used individually or combined for a more comprehensive approach.

Why Use Self-Assessments?

Self-assessments are important in responding to various teen safety issues because they help participants to:

- Become aware of the primary motivators that guide their behavior.
- Explore and learn to "let go" of troublesome habits and behavioral patterns.
- Explore the effects of unconscious childhood messages.
- Gain insight and "a wake-up call" for behavioral change.
- Focus their thinking on behavioral goals for change.
- Uncover resources they possess that can help them to cope better with communications.
- Explore their personal characteristics without judgment.
- Be fully aware of their strengths and weaknesses.

Because the assessments are presented in a straightforward and easy-to-use format, individuals can self-administer, score and interpret each assessment at their own pace.

Introduction for the Participant

You are going to have many different relationships throughout your life. Some of these relationships are with friends, family members, other students in your school, co-workers on your job, and with people in your community like your teachers, grocery store clerks, religious leaders, and members of clubs and organizations to which you belong. As you can see, you will be interacting with some people who have similar communication patterns as you, and some who have very different ways of communicating. You will form some of these relationships very easily, but for some, you may have to work. In order to get along and develop relationships with the various people currently in your life and those you have yet to interact with, you will need a set of communication skills that you can rely on to establish and maintain effective relationships in your life.

Because these relationships are a necessity, not a luxury, you will need to be prepared in order to develop and maintain these critical relationships. Positive, supportive relationships can help you cope with any difficult times you may encounter, reduce the amount of stress you have, and increase your general happiness and life satisfaction. Communication can be described as the center of all interpersonal relationships. The problem is that communication can be very difficult to initiate, develop and maintain. Managing the dynamics of personal relationships can be quite challenging and communication is definitely a skill that takes considerable learning and practice to gain a sense of mastery. Personal relationships are at times difficult to maintain because they are extremely complex, constantly changing and very fragile. That is why it is beneficial to use effective communication skills in personal relationships. Effective communication skills ensure that you will listen actively to what the other person is saying, communicate clearly, negotiate to ensure win-win situations, maintain effective body language and be aware of the cognitive distortions that may block clear communication between two people.

The good news is that if you feel like you are not a good communicator, you can learn and practice the skills that will help your interpersonal relationships grow in effective ways. This book relies on a self-reflective method that is both therapeutic and fun. The *Teen Communication Skills Workbook*, is designed to help you learn about all the various skills that can be used to enhance or block effective communication between you and other people.

Teen Communication Skills Workbook
TABLE OF CONTENTS

TABLE OF CONTENTS

Communi- cation Style

TABLE OF CONTENTS

SECTION I:

Active Listening Scale

Name_____

Date_____

Active Listening Directions

Active listening is a critical piece of any conversation you have with your friends, family, teachers, and anyone else with whom you talk. The Active Listening Scale was designed to help you examine how effective you are in identifying, assessing and overcoming blocks to listening.

This scale consists of two parts; each contains 32 statements.

ACTIVE LISTENING I – **You will think about a person with whom you believe YOU *DO NOT* COMMUNICATE well.**

ACTIVE LISTENING II – **You will think about a person with whom you believe YOU *DO* COMMUNICATE well.**

Read each of the statements and decide whether or not the statement describes you. If the statement describes you, circle the number next to that item under the TRUE column. If the statement does not describe you, circle the number next to that item under the FALSE column.

In the following example from the Active Listening I scale, the circled number under FALSE indicates the statement is not true of the person completing the inventory.

Name a person with whom you believe you *DO NOT* communicate well.

(use name code) MJK

When I am communicating with this person . . .

	TRUE	FALSE
I try to understand what the other person is trying to say	2	(1)

This is not a test and there are no right or wrong answers. Do not spend too much time thinking about your answers. Your initial response will likely be the most true for you. Be sure to respond to every statement.

(Turn to the next page and begin)

Active Listening Scale I

Name a person with whom you believe you _DO NOT_ communicate well.

(use name code) _____

When I am communicating with this person . . .

	TRUE	FALSE
1. I try to understand what the other person is trying to say	2	1
2. I am constantly comparing myself to this person.	1	2
3. I try to read this person's mind	1	2
4. I put aside my judgments of this person	2	1
5. I listen for feelings as well as what is being said	2	1
6. I ask for clarification if I do not understand something	2	1
7. I usually disagree with this person	1	2
8. I agree with what this person says, even if I don't	1	2
9. I go on and on to prove I am right	1	2
10. I make appropriate eye contact.	2	1
11. I hear only what I want to hear	1	2
12. I plan my response while this person is talking	1	2
13. I often repeat what this person says.	2	1
14. I listen with my full attention	2	1
15. I do not concern myself about this person's feelings	1	2
16. I often find myself lying	1	2
17. I attempt to understand the meaning of the words being said	2	1
18. I finish this person's sentences	1	2
19. I think about other things while this person is talking	1	2
20. I jump in and give advice before this person stops talking.	1	2
21. I make jokes or mock the person talking	1	2
22. I ask questions to get further information	2	1
23. I judge this person ahead of time	1	2
24. I reassure and support this person	2	1
25. I try to solve this person's problems for him/her	1	2
26. I am easily distracted	1	2
27. I focus on specific points and shut out the rest of the message.	1	2
28. I notice this person's body language and tone of voice	2	1
29. I find myself daydreaming	1	2
30. I always seem to understand this person's position clearly	2	1
31. I often interrupt this person	1	2
32. I let this person know I heard what was said	2	1

TOTAL = _____

(Continued on the next page)

Active Listening Scale II

Name a person with whom you believe you _DO_ communicate well.

(use name code) _____

When I am communicating with this person . . .

	TRUE	FALSE
1. I try to understand what the other person is trying to say	2	1
2. I am constantly comparing myself to this person	1	2
3. I try to read this person's mind	1	2
4. I put aside my judgments of this person	2	1
5. I listen for feelings as well as what is being said	2	1
6. I ask for clarification if I do not understand something	2	1
7. I usually disagree with this person	1	2
8. I agree with what this person says, even if I don't	1	2
9. I go on and on to prove I am right	1	2
10. I make appropriate eye contact	2	1
11. I hear only what I want to hear	1	2
12. I plan my response while this person is talking	1	2
13. I often repeat what this person says	2	1
14. I listen with my full attention	2	1
15. I do not concern myself about this person's feelings	1	2
16. I often find myself lying	1	2
17. I attempt to understand the meaning of the words being said	2	1
18. I finish this person's sentences	1	2
19. I think about other things while this person is talking	1	2
20. I jump in and give advice before this person stops talking	1	2
21. I make jokes or mock the person talking	1	2
22. I ask questions to get further information	2	1
23. I judge this person ahead of time	1	2
24. I reassure and support this person	2	1
25. I try to solve this person's problems for him/her	1	2
26. I am easily distracted	1	2
27. I focus on specific points and shut out the rest of the message	1	2
28. I notice this person's body language and tone of voice	2	1
29. I find myself daydreaming	1	2
30. I always seem to understand this person's position clearly	2	1
31. I often interrupt this person	1	2
32. I let this person know I heard what was said	2	1

TOTAL = _____

(Go to the Scoring Directions on the next page)

Active Listening Scale
Scoring Directions

The Active Listening Scale will identify how proficient you are at listening to others with whom you are talking. For each of the scales on the previous two pages, add the numbers that you circled and put that number in the TOTAL space at the bottom of each page.

Then, transfer your totals to the spaces below:

ACTIVE LISTENING I – TOTAL   =   _____
(The person with whom you believe you DO NOT communicate well.)

ACTIVE LISTENING II – TOTAL   =   _____
(The person with whom you believe you DO communicate well.)

Profile Interpretation

Individual Scale Score	Indication
56 – 64	You are an active listener with this person. You go out of your way to truly hear what this person is saying, ask questions for more information and repeat important points back to the communicator.
40 – 55	You are an average listener with this person and possibly other people. You could use some help in further developing your listening skills.
32 – 39	You definitely need to further develop your listening skills with this person and probably others as well.

What differences do you notice between your listening skills when you are with someone you get along with and someone you do not.

_____
_____
_____
_____

Better listening skills will help you have better relationships with everyone, whether it's personal, school, work, volunteer or other-related.

Regardless of your score, the exercises and activities that follow are designed to help you increase your listening skills.

Building Your Listening Skills

Active listening sounds easy, doesn't it? Actually, it is quite challenging. It takes commitment, thought and awareness of what keeps you from being a good listener. Effective listening skills will help people to better understand each other.

Being focused on what someone is saying is the most important part of listening.

What Keeps You from Listening Actively?

I. DAYDREAMING

Daydreaming is allowing your attention to wander somewhere else. They are roadblocks to positive communication. It is a time when you stop listening and drift away into your own thoughts. (use name codes)

In what situations have you found yourself daydreaming?
(Ex: Classes that I don't like.)

1. _____
2. _____

What was the person talking about?
(Ex: MYT is giving a history lecture.)

1. _____
2. _____

How do you feel about the other person?
(Ex: She's nice – I'm just not interested in history.)

1. _____
2. _____

How do you think the other person feels?
(Ex: She probably feels bad when she sees me daydreaming.)

1. _____
2. _____

What can you do to prevent this?
(Ex: Maybe I can read ahead and become more interested. Then I can participate.)

1. _____
2. _____

(Continued on the next page)

What Keeps You from Listening Actively? *(Continued)*

II. REHEARSING

Rehearsing is when you are busy thinking about what you are going to say next, so that you never completely hear what the other person is telling you. (use name codes)

In what situations have you found yourself rehearsing?
(Ex: When I know I am going to need to defend my position.)

1. _____

2. _____

What was the conversation about?
(Ex: KMM yelled at me for not getting my chores done.)

1. _____

2. _____

How do you feel about the other person?
(Ex: He's OK – but nags a lot.)

1. _____

2. _____

How do you think the other person feels?
(Ex: He probably gets aggravated with me because I don't listen and then make an excuse.)

1. _____

2. _____

What can you do to prevent this?
(Ex: I guess I could listen to him to find out what he wants from me and then try harder.)

1. _____

2. _____

(Continued on the next page)

What Keeps You from Listening Actively? *(Continued)*

III. FILTERING

Filtering is when you listen to certain parts of the conversation, but not all.

In what situations have you found yourself filtering, listening to only parts of the conversation?

(Ex: When I am with MGG and my cell phone signals that I have a text.)

1. _____

2. _____

What was the topic?

(Ex: It doesn't matter, I like to look at my texts)

1. _____

2. _____

How do you feel about the other person?

(Ex: I love her.)

1. _____

2. _____

How do you think the other person feels?

(Ex: I think she feels like I don't enjoy visiting with her.)

1. _____

2. _____

What can you do to prevent this?

(Ex: I could shut off the phone when I am visiting with her.)

1. _____

2. _____

(Continued on the next page)

What Keeps You from Listening Actively? *(Continued)*

IV. JUDGING

Judging is when you have stopped listening to the other person because you have already judged, placed labels, made assumptions about, or stereotyped the other person.

In what situations have you found yourself judging the person with whom you are communicating?

(Ex: When I know ahead of time that no matter what OMH will say, I will not agree with him.

1. _____
2. _____

What was the person talking about?

(Ex: Politics)

1. _____
2. _____

How do you feel about the other person?

(Ex: I like him a lot, but don't agree with his politics.
I feel he just repeats what other people tell him and doesn't think for himself.)

1. _____
2. _____

How do you think the other person feels?

(Ex: He probably thinks the same thing about me.)

1. _____
2. _____

What can you do to prevent this?

(Ex: Maybe we could agree to disagree but at least ask good questions and listen to each other.)

1. _____
2. _____

(Continued on the next page)

What Keeps You from Listening Actively? *(Continued)*

V. DISTRACTIONS

Distraction occurs when your attention is divided by something internal to you (headaches, worry, hunger) or external to you (traffic, whispering, others talking).

In what situations have you found yourself distracted?
> *(Ex: I was at my volunteer job and someone asked me for help.*
> *I was worrying about MGM and didn't hear the person.)*

1. _____
2. _____

What was the person talking about?
> *(Ex: He needed me to help him with his wheelchair.)*

1. _____
2. _____

How do you feel about the other person?
> *(Ex: He is a very nice man and I felt terrible.)*

1. _____
2. _____

How do you think the other person feels?
> *(Ex: He felt neglected – but understood when I explained.)*

1. _____
2. _____

What can you do to prevent this?
> *(Ex: I have to stay in the here and now, and focus on what I am doing.)*

1. _____
2. _____

Developing Active Listening Skills

Listening is a critical aspect of effective communication. Regardless of your score, the following exercises will help you become a better listener. Try practicing all of the active listening skills that follow, then select and use the one with which you feel most comfortable.

PARAPHRASING

In paraphrasing, you restate, in your own words, what you think the other person just said. You can use such phrases as *"In other words . . ."* or *"What I am hearing you say is . . ."*

In the following spaces, try to paraphrase what the speaker is saying.

What the speaker says	How you could paraphrase
Ex: *"I don't want to date him anymore."*	*"In other words, sounds like you want to break up with him."*
"My father never listens to me."	
"I don't know if I can afford to go to college or not."	
"I can't decide if I should go to the party."	
"I hate school."	

(Continued on the next page)

Developing Active Listening Skills *(Continued)*

REFLECTION OF FEELINGS

In reflection of feelings, you restate what the person has said to you much like paraphrasing. However, in this skill you restate what you think the speaker is feeling.

In the following spaces, try to reflect the feelings of the speaker.

What the speaker says	How you could reflect feelings
Ex: "I don't want to date him anymore."	"You really sound upset with him."
"My father never listens to me."	
"I don't know if I can afford to go to college or not."	
"I can't decide if I should go to the party."	
"I hate school."	

(Continued on the next page)

Developing Active Listening Skills *(Continued)*

CLARIFICATION

In clarification, you tell the other person what you thought you heard, learn whether you were right or wrong, and then ask questions to clarify.

In the following spaces, try to clarify what the speaker is saying.

What the speaker says	How you could clarify what was said
Ex: *"I don't want to date him anymore."*	*"You don't think it's worth trying to work things out?"*
"My father never listens to me."	
"I don't know if I can afford to go to college or not."	
"I can't decide if I should go to the party."	
"I hate school."	

(Continued on the next page)

Developing Active Listening Skills *(Continued)*

OPEN-ENDED QUESTIONS

There are two different types of questions you can ask when you want to hear someone's information. Closed-ended questions are the least effective in that they usually ask for only a simple yes or no answer. An example of a closed-ended question is *"Did you have a good time last night?"* It is better to use open-ended questions. Open-ended questions encourage people to answer questions in greater detail. *"Tell me about your date last night!"*

In the following spaces, try to ask open-ended questions to what the speaker is saying.

What the speaker says	What open-ended questions could you ask?
Ex: *"I don't want to date him anymore."*	*"Tell me more about what happened the last time you went out with him."*
"My father never listens to me."	
"I don't know if I can afford to go to college or not."	
"I can't decide if I should go to the party."	
"I hate school."	

Body Language

Body language is a form of non-verbal communication and represents the message that you are giving by how you hold your body in a conversation. It includes eye movements, gestures, facial expressions, and body posture. Showing active listening through your body language gives the message that you are interested and listening, and encouraging the speaker to tell you more. Some suggestions for effective body language when communicating with others include the following:

- Maintain eye contact (look the person in the eyes, but do not stare . . . look away occasionally).

- Move closer to the person, but do not cross over any personal boundaries.

- Lean forward if you are sitting.

- Nod from time-to-time to show that you understand.

- Say things like "yes" or "uh-huh" to encourage the speaker to continue.

- Keep your posture open to the person by keeping your arms unfolded and uncrossed.

- Keep distractions to a minimum (answering your cell phone, texting, looking at the time, etc.).

- Be aware of your own body language and facial expressions.

When you are communicating with other people, which of the above body language cues do you use?

_____

_____

_____

_____

When you are communicating with other people, which of the above body language cues do you need to use more often?

_____

_____

_____

_____

Listening Strengths and Areas for Growth

What are your strengths when you listen to other people? Which people?
(use name codes)

_____

_____

_____

_____

_____

_____

_____

_____

_____

_____

_____

_____

_____

What are your areas for growth when you listen to other people? Which people?
(use name codes)

_____

_____

_____

_____

_____

_____

_____

_____

_____

_____

_____

_____

_____

Listening and Relationships

Who in your life REALLY listens to you and is interested in what you have to say?
(use name codes)

_____

How do you feel about that?

_____

_____

_____

How does that affect your relationship with that person?

_____

_____

_____

Who in your life does NOT listen to you and does not seem interested in what you have to say?

_____

How do you feel about that?

_____

_____

How does that affect your relationship with that person?

_____

_____

To whom do you actively listen? Why?

_____

_____

To whom do you NOT actively listen? Why not?

_____

_____

_____

Quotations About Listening

The following quotations pertain to listening actively. Respond to the questions.
(use name codes)

> *The most basic of all human needs is the need to understand and be understood. The best way to understand people is to listen to them.*
> **~ Ralph Nichols**

Who doesn't understand you? _____

How can you ask them to listen to you? _____

_____

_____

Who is a person you don't understand? _____

How can you take some time to listen to and try to understand this person? _____

_____

_____

· ·

> *I think the one lesson I have learned is that there is no substitute for paying attention.*
> **~ Diane Sawyer**

In what areas of your life, and with whom, do you not pay attention to what is being said to you? Why?

_____

_____

_____

In what areas of your life, and with whom, do you really pay attention to what is being said to you? Why?

_____

_____

_____

5 Steps of Active Listening

1. Stop what you are doing, sit down and focus. Be aware of body language. Uncross your arms and face the person speaking. This shows you care about what the person is saying.

2. While the other person is talking stop thinking about what you are doing today. You are not listening if you are preparing a response. It is okay to take a minute to respond. It shows that you are thinking about what was said.

3. Really listen! Nod your head. Ask questions to encourage information sharing.

4. Be open-minded to what the person is saying. Do not decide that you disagree before the person stops talking.

5. Repeat what you think the person said if you are not sure that you understand completely. This shows that you are paying attention.

Ways to Improve Communication

- Clarify what you think you hear.

- Paraphrase or repeat what you heard back to the person.

- Reflect feelings you hear behind what the person is saying.

- Use effective body language and watch the other person's body language for how the person is feeling.

- Let the other person talk too.

- Ask open-ended questions.

- Provide feedback but do not interrupt.

- Spend more time listening than talking.

- Do not finish the other person's sentences.

- Plan responses after the other person finishes speaking.

- Listen actively.

SECTION II:

Nonverbal Communication Scale

Name_____

Date_____

Nonverbal Communication Scale Directions

Learning to communicate is a critical life skill. Communication is the process of sending and receiving messages that allow people to share information, ideas and knowledge. Most people think of communication as speaking to someone, but communication actually has two components – verbal and nonverbal. Nonverbal communication can be defined as communication without words and includes such behaviors as facial expressions, touching, gestures, posture, body language and spatial distance between two people.

The Nonverbal Communication Scale can help you identify the ways that you communicate nonverbally. This scale contains four sections with twenty statements in each section. In each section, select a person with whom you spend a lot of time and write his or her name code. Read each of the statements and decide if the statement is true or false. If it is true, circle the word TRUE next to the statement. If the statement is false, circle the word FALSE next to the statement. Ignore the numbers after the TRUE and FALSE choices. They are for scoring purposes and will be used later. Finish all of the items before going back to score this scale.

In the following example, the circled FALSE indicates that the item is false for the participant completing the scale:

SECTION I: FAMILY MEMBERS

When talking with this family member (name code) _____*MMJ*_____

  1. I maintain steady eye contact while speaking . . . . True (0) (False)(1)   Score _____

This is not a test and there are no right or wrong answers. Do not spend too much time thinking about your answers. Your initial response will likely be the most true for you. Be sure to respond to every statement.

(Turn to the next page and begin)

Nonverbal Communication Scale

Section I: Family Members

When talking with this family member . . . (name code) _____

1. I maintain steady eye contact while speaking. . . . . True (0)   False (1)   Score _____

2. I yawn or show other signs of boredom . . . . True (0)   False (1)   Score _____

3. I show no facial expression. . . . . True (0)   False (1)   Score _____

4. I greet him or her warmly . . . . True (1)   False (0)   Score _____

5. I nod my head a lot to confirm what the person is saying . . True (1)   False (0)   Score _____

6. I turn my head away due to distractions. . . . . True (0)   False (1)   Score _____

7. I avoid rolling my eyes . . . . True (1)   False (0)   Score _____

8. I have a relaxed posture . . . . True (1)   False (0)   Score _____

9. I often lean toward the other person to express interest . . . True (1)   False (0)   Score _____

10. I cross my arms across my chest . . . . True (0)   False (1)   Score _____

11. I tap my fingers or feet . . . . True (0)   False (1)   Score _____

12. I do not clench my fists when I'm angry . . . . True (1)   False (0)   Score _____

13. I look at my watch or a clock when he or she is talking . . . . True (0)   False (1)   Score _____

14. I put my hands on my hips . . . . True (0)   False (1)   Score _____

15. I stand tall and straight. . . . . True (1)   False (0)   Score _____

16. I make appropriate physical contact
    (pat on back, touch arm). . . . . True (1)   False (0)   Score _____

17. I text while he or she is talking . . . . True (0)   False (1)   Score _____

18. I answer the phone during an important conversation . . . . True (0)   False (1)   Score _____

19. I shake my head from side to side, as if in disgust. . . . . . . True (0)   False (1)   Score _____

20. I try not to fidget . . . . True (1)   False (0)   Score _____

TOTAL I. _____

(Continued on the next page)

Nonverbal Communication Scale *(Continued)*

Section II: Friends

When talking with a friend . . . (name code) _____

  1. I maintain steady eye contact while speaking . . . . True (1)   False (0)   Score _____

  2. I yawn or show other signs of boredom . . . . True (0)   False (1)   Score _____

  3. I show no facial expression. . . . . True (0)   False (1)   Score _____

  4. I greet him or her warmly . . . . True (1)   False (0)   Score _____

  5. I nod my head a lot to confirm what the person is saying . . True (1)   False (0)   Score _____

  6. I turn my head away due to distractions. . . . . True (0)   False (1)   Score _____

  7. I avoid rolling my eyes . . . . True (1)   False (0)   Score _____

  8. I have a relaxed posture . . . . True (1)   False (0)   Score _____

  9. I often lean toward the other person to express interest . . . True (1)   False (0)   Score _____

10. I cross my arms across my chest . . . . True (0)   False (1)   Score _____

11. I tap my fingers or feet. . . . . True (0)   False (1)   Score _____

12. I do not clench my fists when I'm angry . . . . True (1)   False (0)   Score _____

13. I look at my watch or a clock when he or she is talking . . . . True (0)   False (1)   Score _____

14. I put my hands on my hips. . . . . True (0)   False (1)   Score _____

15. I stand tall and straight. . . . . True (1)   False (0)   Score _____

16. I make appropriate physical contact
    (pat on back, touch arm). . . . . True (1)   False (0)   Score _____

17. I text while he or she is talking . . . . True (0)   False (1)   Score _____

18. I answer the phone during an important conversation . . . . True (0)   False (1)   Score _____

19. I shake my head from side to side, as if in disgust . . . . True (0)   False (1)   Score _____

20. I try not to fidget . . . . True (1)   False (0)   Score _____

TOTAL II. _____

(Continued on the next page)

Nonverbal Communication Scale (Continued)

Section III: Community Members

When talking with a member of my community . . . (name code) _____

1. I maintain steady eye contact while speaking. . . . . True (1)   False (0)   Score _____

2. I yawn or show other signs of boredom . . . . True (0)   False (1)   Score _____

3. I show no facial expression. . . . . True (0)   False (1)   Score _____

4. I greet him or her warmly . . . . True (1)   False (0)   Score _____

5. I nod my head a lot to confirm what the person is saying . . True (1)   False (0)   Score _____

6. I turn my head away due to distractions. . . . . True (0)   False (1)   Score _____

7. I avoid rolling my eyes . . . . True (1)   False (0)   Score _____

8. I have a relaxed posture . . . . True (1)   False (0)   Score _____

9. I often lean toward the other person to express interest . . . True (1)   False (0)   Score _____

10. I cross my arms across my chest . . . . True (0)   False (1)   Score _____

11. I tap my fingers or feet . . . . True (0)   False (1)   Score _____

12. I do not clench my fists when I'm angry . . . . True (1)   False (0)   Score _____

13. I look at my watch or a clock when he or she is talking . . . . True (0)   False (1)   Score _____

14. I put my hands on my hips . . . . True (0)   False (1)   Score _____

15. I stand tall and straight. . . . . True (1)   False (0)   Score _____

16. I make appropriate physical contact
    (pat on back, touch arm). . . . . True (1)   False (0)   Score _____

17. I text while he or she is talking . . . . True (0)   False (1)   Score _____

18. I answer the phone during an important conversation . . . . True (0)   False (1)   Score _____

19. I shake my head from side to side, as if in disgust. . . . . . . True (0)   False (1)   Score _____

20. I try not to fidget . . . . True (1)   False (0)   Score _____

TOTAL III. _____

(Continued on the next page)

Nonverbal Communication Scale *(Continued)*

Section IV: Someone at school, work or volunteer place

When talking with this person . . . (name code) _____

1. I maintain steady eye contact while speaking . . . . True (1)   False (0)   Score _____

2. I yawn or show other signs of boredom . . . . True (0)   False (1)   Score _____

3. I show no facial expression. . . . . True (0)   False (1)   Score _____

4. I greet him or her warmly . . . . True (1)   False (0)   Score _____

5. I nod my head a lot to confirm what the person is saying . . True (1)   False (0)   Score _____

6. I turn my head away due to distractions. . . . . True (0)   False (1)   Score _____

7. I avoid rolling my eyes . . . . True (1)   False (0)   Score _____

8. I have a relaxed posture . . . . True (1)   False (0)   Score _____

9. I often lean toward the other person to express interest . . . True (1)   False (0)   Score _____

10. I cross my arms across my chest . . . . True (0)   False (1)   Score _____

11. I tap my fingers or feet . . . . True (0)   False (1)   Score _____

12. I do not clench my fists when I'm angry . . . . True (1)   False (0)   Score _____

13. I look at my watch or a clock when he or she is talking . . . . True (0)   False (1)   Score _____

14. I put my hands on my hips . . . . True (0)   False (1)   Score _____

15. I stand tall and straight. . . . . True (1)   False (0)   Score _____

16. I make appropriate physical contact
    (pat on back, touch arm) . . . . True (1)   False (0)   Score _____

17. I text while he or she is talking . . . . True (0)   False (1)   Score _____

18. I answer the phone during an important conversation   . . True (0)   False (1)   Score _____

19. I shake my head from side to side, as if in disgust . . . . True (0)   False (1)   Score _____

20. I try not to fidget . . . . True (1)   False (0)   Score _____

TOTAL IV. _____

(Go to the Scoring Directions on the next page)

Nonverbal Communication Scale
Scoring Directions

The Nonverbal Communication Scale will help you identify how you communication through your body language in social situations. To score this scale, you need to determine your scores on each of the individual scales and for the overall nonverbal communication total.

To score the scale, look at the items you just completed. Add the numbers after each choice rather than the TRUE or FALSE. Total your score for each section.

Use the spaces below to transfer your scores to each of the scales below. Then total the scores and put that number in the TOTAL column.

    I. Family Members Scale   _____

    II. Friends Scale   _____

    III. Community Members Scale   _____

    IV. School, Work or Volunteer Place Scale   _____

Profile Interpretation

Individual Scale Score	Result	Indications
0 to 6	Low	You probably show poor body language when communicating with other people and do not maintain good posture, use appropriate facial expressions, keep a proper distance when communicating and/or maintain eye contact.
7 to 13	Moderate	You show good body language when communicating with other people. You usually maintain good posture, use appropriate facial expressions, keep a proper distance when communicating and maintain eye contact.
14 to 20	High	You show excellent body language when communicating with other people. You maintain tall and straight posture, use appropriate facial expressions, keep an effective distance when communicating and maintain good eye contact.

The higher your score on the Nonverbal Communication Scale, the more apt you are to show good nonverbal communication when talking with other people. In the areas in which you score in the **Moderate** or **Low** range you should make efforts to use better nonverbal communication skills when speaking with others.

No matter if you scored **Low**, **Moderate** or **High**, the exercises and activities that follow are designed to help you explore your nonverbal communication skills in various roles you play in life.

Exploring Nonverbal Communication With Your Family Members

Complete the following questions about how you show nonverbal communication with members of your family. (use name codes)

How has your nonverbal communication affected your relationships with family members in a positive way?

_____

_____

_____

How has your nonverbal communication affected your relationships with family members in a negative way?

_____

_____

_____

How has your nonverbal communication been misinterpreted by members of your family?

_____

_____

_____

How does your nonverbal communication with members of your family show or hide how you are truly feeling at the time?

_____

_____

_____

What nonverbal communication patterns can you identify?

_____

_____

_____

Exploring Nonverbal Communication With Your Friends

Complete the following questions about how you show nonverbal communication with your friends. (use name codes)

How has your nonverbal communication affected your relationships with your friends in a positive way?

_____

_____

_____

How has your nonverbal communication affected your relationships with your friends in a negative way?

_____

_____

_____

How has your nonverbal communication been misinterpreted by your friends?

_____

_____

_____

How does your nonverbal communication with your friends show or hide how you are truly feeling at the time?

_____

_____

_____

What nonverbal communication patterns can you identify?

_____

_____

_____

Exploring Nonverbal Communication
With Members of Your Community

Complete the following questions about how you show nonverbal communication with members of your community. (use name codes)

How has your nonverbal communication affected your relationships with members of your community in a positive way?

_____

_____

_____

How has your nonverbal communication affected your relationships with members of your community in a negative way?

_____

_____

_____

How has your nonverbal communication been misinterpreted by members of your community?

_____

_____

_____

How does your nonverbal communication with members of your community show or hide how you are truly feeling at the time?

_____

_____

_____

What nonverbal communication patterns can you identify?

_____

_____

_____

Exploring Nonverbal Communication With People at School or Volunteer/ Work Place

Complete the following questions about how you show nonverbal communication with people at school or volunteer and work place. (use name codes)

How has your nonverbal communication affected your relationships with people at school or volunteer/work place in a positive way?

_____

_____

_____

How has your nonverbal communication affected your relationships with people at school or volunteer/work place in a negative way?

_____

_____

_____

How has your nonverbal communication been misinterpreted by people at school or volunteer/work place?

_____

_____

_____

How does your nonverbal communication with people at school or volunteer/work place show or hide how you are truly feeling at the time?

_____

_____

_____

What nonverbal communication patterns can you identify?

_____

_____

_____

Tips for Nonverbal Communication

Following are some tips for improving your nonverbal communication when talking with other people. Remember that people from different cultures may show some variations of these behaviors.

- Always welcome people with a warm, firm handshake.

- Find comfortable personal space when talking to another person. How close you get may depend on your relationship with the other person. The better you know someone, the closer you can stand when talking. Avoid being too close or too far away.

- Be relaxed and listen attentively to others. You can be a good listener and show positive attention by slightly leaning your body forward. This will show the other person that you are interested in the conversation.

- Maintain frequent eye contact at a comfortable level. Avoid staring, glaring or looking away.

- Provide nonverbal cues to the other person by nodding your head in approval, smiling and looking interested.

- Keep gestures simple and unobtrusive.

- Stay alert when communicating with others. Closing your eyes, yawning or looking at your watch can show disinterest or boredom.

- Be aware of where you place your arms when talking. By crossing your arms across your chest, you appear to be closed to what other people are saying.

- Make appropriate physical contact with other people. Be aware of when it is appropriate to hug, kiss and touch other people.

- Stand tall and straight; do not slouch.

- _____

- _____

- _____

- _____

Nonverbal Communication Identification

In the following table, look at the nonverbal communication in the left-hand column. In the right-hand column, write what you think the nonverbal communication means.

Nonverbal Communication	What does it mean?
Failing to maintain eye contact	
Standing erect, but not rigid	
Leaning slightly forward	
Tapping your fingers	
Nodding your head when listening	
Using your hands to gesture	
Clenching your fists	
Rolling your eyes	
Shaking hands warmly	
Crossing arms across chest	
Looking at your watch	
Yawning	

Nonverbal Communication Log

Think about a past situation that occurred in which you think you, or the other person, could have improved the nonverbal skills. Complete the following log to learn more about your nonverbal communication. (use name codes)

Situation: _____

_____

_____

_____

_____

_____

_____

_____

Name code of the person with whom you were conversing: _____

This person's relationship to you: _____

_____

_____

What was your conversation about?

_____

_____

_____

_____

_____

_____

_____

_____

(Continued on next page)

Nonverbal Communication Log *(Continued)*

Describe this person's body language.

_____

_____

_____

What message did it give to you?

_____

_____

_____

Describe your body language.

_____

_____

_____

What message did it give to this person?

_____

_____

_____

How do you think body language of both of you influenced the way you both felt about the situation or your attitudes?

_____

_____

_____

_____

What could you both have done differently?

_____

_____

_____

Nonverbal Communications Pitfalls

What nonverbal communication pitfalls do you make the most often? Why?

_____

_____

_____

_____

_____

_____

_____

_____

_____

_____

_____

_____

How can you begin to improve your nonverbal communication when interacting with others?

_____

_____

_____

_____

_____

_____

_____

_____

_____

_____

_____

_____

_____

A Communication Quotation

"The most important thing in communication is hearing what isn't said."
~ Peter F. Drucker

Write a short story about a time when the above quotation was obvious to you in a conversation you had with someone. Remember to use name codes.

_____

_____

_____

_____

_____

_____

_____

_____

_____

_____

_____

_____

_____

_____

_____

_____

_____

_____

_____

_____

_____

_____

_____

Conversation and Nonverbals

Here are two examples of verbal communications not matching the nonverbal communication that is happening at the same time.

1. *Angry, making fists and red in the face but continuing with a pleasant conversation.*

2. *Saying "I'm interested to know more" but looking around and watching the clock.*

List other examples of some of your non-verbal behaviors.

_____

_____

_____

_____

_____

_____

_____

_____

_____

_____

Now list some non-verbal behaviors you have observed.

_____

_____

_____

_____

_____

_____

_____

_____

_____

_____

Improving
Nonverbal Communication

- Be aware of your nonverbal communication so you can be a better receiver of messages.

- Send signals that reinforce your understanding of what is being said.

- Use effective nonverbal communication to solidify your relationship with others.

- Learn about the nonverbal cues of friends from cultures other than your own.

Nonverbal Communications

POSITIVE

Arms relaxed on table or chair arms

Attentive listening

Eye contact

Facing person

Facial expressions showing interest

Hands relaxed and open

Firm handshake

Leaning towards a person

Maintaining physical boundaries

Nodding in agreement

Open gestures

Posture tall and straight

Relaxed demeanor

Smiling appropriately

Tilting head

Touching appropriately

NEGATIVE

Blank facial expression

Clenched fist

Crossed arms

Eye rolls

Fake smile

Fidgeting

Finger pointing

Frequent looking away

Frowning

Guarded expression

Hands on hips

Head shaking side to side

Inappropriate touch

Legs swinging

Looking at the clock

Negative hand gestures

Pouting

Scowling

Shaking legs or feet

Shoulders shrugging

Slumped posture

Texting while talking

Turning head away

Yawning

SECTION III:
Communication Skills Scale

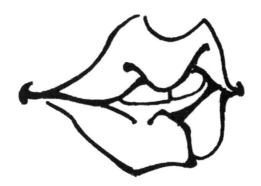

Name_____

Date_____

Communication Skills Scale
Directions

Communication skills are very important for developing and maintaining good and lasting relationships with others. The Communications Skills Scale can help you explore how well you will do when you are interacting with other people. This assessment contains 44 statements. Read each of the statements and decide how much you agree. In each of the choices listed, circle the number of your response on the line to the right of each statement. Ignore the number; just respond whether it is very true, somewhat true or not true.

In the following example, the circled 1 indicates that the statement is not true of the person completing the scale.

	VERY TRUE	SOMEWHAT TRUE	NOT TRUE
1. I try not to give the message of boredom by daydreaming	3	2	(1)

This is not a test and there are no right or wrong answers. Do not spend too much time thinking about your answers. Your initial response will likely be the most true for you. Be sure to respond to every statement.

(Turn to the next page and begin)

Communication Skills Scale

	VERY TRUE	SOMEWHAT TRUE	NOT TRUE
1. I try not to give the message of boredom by daydreaming	3	2	1
2. When a conversation turns to feelings, I often change the subject	1	2	3
3. I am afraid to hurt the feelings of others	1	2	3
4. I am good at reading the other person's body language	3	2	1
5. I know how to talk so that people can understand	3	2	1
6. I do not like to discuss personal issues	1	2	3
7. I am not afraid to express an opinion that is different	3	2	1
8. I finish other peoples' sentences for them	1	2	3
9. People do not always get what I am trying to say	1	2	3
10. My emotions generally match my words	3	2	1
11. If I need to, I will stand up for myself	3	2	1
12. I let others speak without interrupting them	3	2	1
13. I judge people within five minutes of meeting them	1	2	3
14. I have trouble talking about my feelings	1	2	3
15. I am not as assertive as I could be	1	2	3
16. I ask questions when I do not understand something	3	2	1
17. I have difficulty showing my feelings	1	2	3
18. I often become angry when talking to others	1	2	3
19. I have trouble asking for what I need	1	2	3
20. I often pretend to listen, even though my mind wanders	1	2	3
21. I ask people if they understand what I am saying	3	2	1
22. I can detect the emotional moods of others	3	2	1

(Continued on the next page)

Communication Skills Scale *(Continued)*

	VERY TRUE	SOMEWHAT TRUE	NOT TRUE
23. I am okay expressing opinions that are different from others	3	2	1
24. I rarely jump to conclusions.	3	2	1
25. I use "I" statements when I give feedback to others.	3	2	1
26. I get upset if others disagree with me	1	2	3
27. I do not like to say things that offend other people.	1	2	3
28. I have trouble identifying the hidden meanings behind what is said	1	2	3
29. I ask for feedback about what I say	3	2	1
30. I raise my voice, even though I am not aware of it at the time	1	2	3
31. I ask questions so I will not look foolish	1	2	3
32. I try to put myself in the speaker's shoes.	3	2	1
33. I communicate with my body language to match what I am saying	3	2	1
34. I avoid situations in which people get emotional.	1	2	3
35. I do not hesitate to tell others how I feel	3	2	1
36. I get distracted easily.	1	2	3
37. I often have to repeat what I say	1	2	3
38. I often change the subject when discussing touchy topics	1	2	3
39. I do not admit if I am angry with someone	1	2	3
40. I rehearse what I will say while people are talking to me.	1	2	3
41. I only speak for myself, not for what "they" said	3	2	1
42. I can solve problems without getting emotional	3	2	1
43. I cannot express my opinions if others don't agree with me	1	2	3
44. I listen to bits and pieces of most conversations	1	2	3

(Go to the Scoring Directions on the next page)

Communication Skills Scale
Scoring Directions

The Communication Skills Scale is designed to measure how well you are able to communicate with other people.

Four important aspects of communicating effectively:

- sending accurate messages
- controlling and discussing emotions
- being assertive when you need to and
- listening actively to what others are saying

These make up the four scales on the assessment. Scales are used to group items and help you to explore your specific communication skills more easily.

Scoring the assessment is very easy. Look at the questions you just answered. Use the spaces below to record the number that you circled on each individual item of the assessment.

(Read across.) Calculate the totals for each of the columns (scales) and put that total underneath each column. Then total your four individual scores to find your grand total.

SCALE I	SCALE II	SCALE III	SCALE IV
1_____	2_____	3_____	4_____
5_____	6_____	7_____	8_____
9_____	10_____	11_____	12_____
13_____	14_____	15_____	16_____
17_____	18_____	19_____	20_____
21_____	22_____	23_____	24_____
25_____	26_____	27_____	28_____
29_____	30_____	31_____	32_____
33_____	34_____	35_____	36_____
37_____	38_____	39_____	40_____
41_____	42_____	43_____	44_____

I. Total		II. Total		III. Total		IV. Total		Grand Total
_____	+	_____	+	_____	+	_____	=	_____
Messages		**Emotions**		**Assertiveness**		**Listening**		

Communication Skills Scale

Communication is an exchange of thoughts, opinions or information. It affects how you handle conflict situations, the level of your self-esteem, your ability to manage situations and how you adjust socially in life. This assessment helps you explore four critical factors in communication.

Profile Interpretation

Individual Scale Score	Total Score for all Four Scales	Result	Indications
11 - 18	44 – 73	Low	You do not, at this point in time, have good communication skills. Be open to learn new and different ways to develop useful communication skills.
19 – 25	74 - 102	Moderate	You have pretty good communication skills, but you could use some improvement. Think of ways to incorporate better communication skills into your conversations with other people.
26 – 33	103 - 132	High	You use excellent communication skills a great deal of the time. Continue to use and improve them in the future.

Regardless of your score on the Communication Skills Scale, low, moderate or high, you will benefit from doing all of the following exercises which have been designed to help you improve your communication skills.

I. Sending Clear Messages

Miscommunication is the cause of many arguments and fights. Working on specific communications skills will help you send clear messages that can be understood by other people. Remember the following:

- When sending messages, use words like I, me, and my to communicate your message. In this way, you own your messages that you share with other people. The use of words like they or some people are ineffective ways to communicate to others. Speak for yourself!

- If you hold in your feelings, small arguments often flare up into larger fights. Look at the person and speak to him or her directly. Assertively express your emotions using "I" statements such as "I get frustrated when you expect me to get all A's."

See examples below of how to express your feelings. In the boxes on the left-hand side of the table, list people to whom you would like to express your feelings. In the right-hand column, express your feelings to that person. (use name codes)

I Would Like to Express My Feelings to ...	What I Would Like To Say ...
Ex: MWM	*I feel frustrated when you expect me to do chores, baby sit and still get all A's.*
Ex: SLG	*I feel angry when you expect me to cheat and do your homework.*

II. Emotions

When you are talking with your friends, try to express yourself by sending emotional messages. This can be difficult because it may pressure you to disclose personal information about yourself, which can feel very risky. Disclose only what you are comfortable saying. Below, write the emotional messages you would like to send to other people. (use name codes)

*Ex: " JKD , **I get scared when you** drive when you've been drinking. I had a relative who had a terrible accident driving when drinking, and I don't want that to happen to you or to me."*

"_____ , **I get scared when you** _____

_____

_____

_____ "

"_____ , **I feel hurt when you** _____

_____

_____

_____ "

"_____ , **I feel unappreciated when you** _____

_____

_____

_____ "

"_____ , **I am sad when you** _____

_____

_____

_____ "

"_____ , **I get excited when you** _____

_____

_____

_____ "

III. Assertiveness

What Do I Want?

By establishing what it is you really want, you will be able to assert yourself when you need to. You will know what is worth passionately pursuing and what to simply walk away from.

In each of the boxes below, list what you want in each of the categories.

(use name codes)

Ex: In School	*I am not getting along with my teacher, GLM, and I'm always in trouble. I need to try harder.*
In School	
At Home	
At Work	
In the Community	
With Friends	
Other	

(Continued on the next page)

III. Assertiveness *(Continued)*

We all have the right to express our desires, needs and wants and expect other people to treat us with respect and dignity. People who are aggressive, passive and assertive have different styles and results:

- People who are AGGRESSIVE infringe on the rights of others and express their feelings through insults, sarcasm, hostile statements and put-downs. They ask or say what they want in a threatening, loud or humiliating way that usually offends others.

- People who are PASSIVE do not express their own needs and feelings, or express them so weakly that people do not pay attention.

- People who are ASSERTIVE describe their feelings and thoughts directly to other people in an honest, open and direct way that enables them to act in their own best interest, stand up for themselves and exercise their personal rights without denying the rights of others.

Assertive communication takes some practice. Complete the following statements.
(use name codes)

In what ways do you have a difficult time expressing your desires, needs and wants?

_____

_____

_____

How has being aggressive caused problems for you . . .

with your friends or at school?

_____

_____

_____

with family?

_____

_____

_____

other people or places?

_____

_____

_____

How has being passive caused problems for you . . .

Identify the people with whom you are passive and do not express your own needs and feelings, or express them so weakly that people do not pay attention.

(use name codes)

People with whom I Am Passive	How I Am Passive
Ex: Family Member SYV	I do whatever I am told to do, no matter how unreasonable it is, and then go in my room and cry.
Family Member	
Boy/Girl Friend	
People I Work with	
Peers	
Sales Clerks	
Religious Leaders	
Authority Figures	
Neighbors	
Large Groups	
Work Supervisors	
Volunteer Supervisors	
Other	

Passive? Aggressive? Assertive?

What style have you used for various situations – and how?

Situations	I Was Passive	I Was Aggressive	I Was Assertive
Ex: Saying NO	*I say yes to everything.*		
Ex: Saying NO		*I yell, "Don't bother me, I'm busy."*	
Ex: Saying NO			*I say, "I wish I could but I'm over-extended."*
Saying NO to others			
Asking for favors			
Disagreeing with others' opinions			
Taking charge of a situation			
Social situations			
Responding to insults			

(Continued on the next page)

Passive? Aggressive? Assertive? *(Continued)*

Situations	I Was Passive	I Was Aggressive	I Was Assertive
Stating my opinion			
Dealing with bullies			
Dating situations			
Taking time for myself			
Speaking in front of groups			
Other			
Other			
Other			

IV. LISTENING

Active listening involves an awareness of what another person is saying to you or asking you to do. Use your active listening skills to make sure that you understand the true meaning of the request or statement. Following are some of the blocks to listening:

INADEQUATE LISTENING – It is easy to get distracted when other people are talking. This includes such things as being too involved with your own thoughts, thinking about your own needs and problems or being too eager to help the other person. It might be that the other person is very different from you.

List times when you become easily distracted when listening to others:

_____

_____

_____

To what specific people do you find it hard to listen? (use name codes)

_____

_____

_____

JUDGMENTAL LISTENING – Listening with the intent of making a judgment about a person can hinder your ability to listen to them. You may find that you are judging what the person is saying as good or bad, right or wrong; you are not listening with empathy. It is important to set aside your criticisms about the person until you can better understand him or her, his or her world and point of view.

List times when you feel you start to judge the other person:

_____

_____

_____

What specific people do find yourself evaluating? (use name codes)

_____

_____

_____

(Continued next page)

IV. LISTENING *(Continued)*

DAYDREAMING – Everyone's attention will wander from time to time. If you find yourself having a difficult time listening to someone, it is probably a sign that you are avoiding or are uninterested in the person or certain topics of conversation.

List times when you feel your attention wandering:

_____

_____

_____

When your mind wanders, which specific people are you talking to? Why does it happen? (use name codes)

_____

_____

_____

REHEARSING – Any time you think "How should I respond to what this person is saying?" you distract yourself from what the person says. As you get better at active listening, your response just comes naturally. It is best to listen intently to the person, the themes, and messages related to their words. Then allow your intuition to provide you with a response.

List times when you find yourself rehearsing what you will say in conversations:

_____

_____

_____

Which specific people are you talking with when you find yourself rehearsing your conversation? (use name codes)

_____

_____

_____

Being More Assertive

How are you going to be more assertive?
With which people and in what situations? (use name codes)

Family:_____

_____

_____

_____

_____

_____

Friends:_____

_____

_____

_____

_____

_____

Teachers: _____

_____

_____

_____

_____

_____

My Work, Volunteer, Job or My Community:_____

_____

_____

_____

_____

_____

My Communication Goals

For the table that follows, list some short-term and some long-term goals you have for improving your communication skills. (use name codes)

Areas of Communication	My Short-Term Goals	My Long-Term Goals
Ex: Messages	I will use 'I' and speak for myself when talking and explaining my feelings with MGF.	I want to have a much better relationship with him some day.
Messages		
Emotions		
Assertiveness		
Listening		

Social Media

Email, texting, blogging and social networking are the most popular social media forms with teens, and for this reason they often lead to major problems.

For example, the underlying tone of a message may be misinterpreted for a variety of reasons:

- If the parties involved in the communications are in different emotional states of mind, the slightest disagreement can quickly spiral out of control leading to a full blown argument. Communication breakdown occurs when you do not communicate well and the written emotion gets lost in translation.

- When teens write messages using phrases to characterize emotions that would normally be delivered via physical body language, the intended message could be misunderstood by the reader due to a complete misinterpretation of the writer's emotional tone.

- Intentional sarcasm in a message only makes matters worse. Emotions portrayed can be interpreted differently when read by different people and often lead to misunderstandings.

- Gossip, flirting, sexting, bullying and threats in social networking can lead to devastating results. Teens need to accept personal responsibility to use this media in a way that does not hurt anyone, including themselves, and to refuse to forward anyone else's messages that can be damaging to others.

Following are some reminders for teens sending an email, text, or blog, or using any form of social networking:

1. **Be clear. Be brief.** Write short messages with a crystal clear point. Do not write long-winded confusing paragraphs that leave room for misinterpretation. Be clear and accurate.

2. **Proofread.** Proofread your message multiple times. Read it aloud. If the message deals with touchy subject matter, have a third-party read it over as well. This can give you added perspective on how well it will be received by the intended recipient. If you would not want anyone else to read this message, DO NOT SEND IT!

3. **Wait.** Write the message, proofread it and then sit on it for a little while before sending it. Come back to it and read it again carefully and out loud. If your emotions were flaring when you wrote the message, a little time can allow these emotions to settle, and you will be able to evaluate the message in a different light.

Pick up the phone! While emailing, texting, blogging and social networking can be convenient, certain discussions need to be handled over the phone, or if possible, in person. If you notice that the situation is starting to deteriorate, don't send another email; it's time to pick up the phone or arrange a face-to-face meeting.

A Quote to Think About

> *"Examine what is said, not who speaks."*
>
> **~ Arabian Proverb**

What does this quote mean to you?

_____

_____

_____

_____

_____

_____

_____

Do you agree with this quote or not? Why?

_____

_____

_____

_____

_____

_____

_____

_____

How can you practice what the quote suggests?

_____

_____

_____

_____

_____

_____

_____

_____

Communication Styles

A person with a passive communication style ...

- speaks quietly
- avoids eye contact
- slumps
- agrees to things against his or her better judgment
- backs down from confrontation
- doesn't express personal needs
- expresses needs weakly and people do not pay attention
- gets 'stepped-on'
- builds up resentment

A person with an assertive communication style ...

- describes feelings and thoughts in an open, honest and direct manner
- speaks clearly
- shows respect for self and others
- makes eye contact
- appears relaxed
- speaks his or her own point of view
- does not deny the rights or opinions of others
- speaks firmly
- is able to say no

A person with an aggressive communication style ...

- clenches his or her jaw or fists
- points out the flaws in others
- threatens
- humiliates others
- speaks loudly and yells at others
- bossy, pushy and sometimes abusive
- dominates and intimidates people
- violates others rights with power, position and language
- bullies

SECTION IV:

Diversity Communication Scale

Name_____

Date_____

Diversity Communication Scale
Directions

Diversity is how we are all different from one another. Your entire life will be filled with relationships that are diverse because of differences in:

- age
- body/size
- class or social standing
- culture
- emotional sensitivity
- ethnicity

- family
- gender
- mental health
- physical abilities and disabilities
- race

- religion
- sexuality
- spirituality
- talents
- values
- other differences

It is important to move past prejudice, bigotry and labeling. Become aware of people as individuals, and accept and understand people who are different from you. Recognize the differences in how people communicate.

The Diversity Communication Scale can help you identify how effectively you are able to develop a rapport with people with whom you have a relationship regardless of the differences between you. This scale contains 36 statements. Read each of the statements and decide how much you agree with the statement. In each of the choices listed, circle your response on the line to the right of each statement.

In the following example, the circled "Like Me" indicates that the statement describes the person taking the assessment:

SECTION I: Valuing Diversity

About people who are different from me:

I-1 I find it interesting to meet people different than me . . . . (Like Me)   Not Like Me

This is not a test and there are no right or wrong answers. Do not spend too much time thinking about your answers. Your initial response will likely be the most true for you. Be sure to respond to every statement.

(Turn to the next page and begin)

Diversity Communication Scale

SECTION I: Valuing Diversity

About people who are different from me:

I-1 I find it interesting to meet people different than me . . . . Like Me   Not Like Me

I-2 I like to be their ally . . . . Like Me   Not Like Me

I-3 I think about whether I have biases about them . . . . Like Me   Not Like Me

I-4 I am accepting of our differences . . . . Like Me   Not Like Me

I-5 I don't expect anyone to be exactly like me . . . . Like Me   Not Like Me

I-6 I like learning about another family's customs . . . . Like Me   Not Like Me

I-7 I like to share and talk about my heritage. . . . . Like Me   Not Like Me

I-8 I find that people with disabilities are courageous . . . . Like Me   Not Like Me

I-9 I do not label anyone . . . . Like Me   Not Like Me

I-10 I ask people about their differences and tell them about mine . . . . Like Me   Not Like Me

I-11 I have relationships with people different from me . . . . Like Me   Not Like Me

I-12 I try to be very sensitive when talking with people different
from me to be sure I don't hurt their feelings . . . . Like Me   Not Like Me

(Continued on the next page)

Diversity Communication Scale

SECTION II: Communicating Across Cultures

About people who are different from me:

II-1 I enjoy talking with them and noticing our differences . . . . Like Me   Not Like Me

II-2 I like learning about them and respect their culture . . . . Like Me   Not Like Me

II-3 I am patient when talking to them . . . . Like Me   Not Like Me

II-4 I take time to listen actively to what they say . . . . Like Me   Not Like Me

II-5 I understand that they may not communicate
in the same way I do. . . . . Like Me   Not Like Me

II-6 I notice differences in communication styles and values and
I don't assume that my way is the right way. . . . . Like Me   Not Like Me

II-7 I am attentive to the messages being sent through body language,
especially when the language cues are different from mine . . . . . . Like Me   Not Like Me

II-8 I often repeat what they say to make sure I understand them . . . . Like Me   Not Like Me

II-9 I never assume they are using words and phrases the way I do . . . Like Me   Not Like Me

II-10 I maintain an appropriate distance when speaking. . . . . Like Me   Not Like Me

II-11 I don't assume that my way is the right way to communicate . . . . Like Me   Not Like Me

II-12 I avoid behavior that shows disrespect to others . . . . Like Me   Not Like Me

(Continued on the next page)

Diversity Communication Scale (Continued)

SECTION III: EMPATHY

About people who are different from me:

III-1 I help each person to identify the feelings that are
being experienced . . . . Like Me   Not Like Me

III-2 I am aware that I may not understand what they are saying
and then I ask for clarification . . . . Like Me   Not Like Me

III-3 I am usually able to catch on to what the person is hinting at. . . . Like Me   Not Like Me

III-4 I know that they may not be able to explain everything
clearly to me . . . . Like Me   Not Like Me

III-5 I try to feel the intensity of their emotions. . . . . Like Me   Not Like Me

III-6 I think they are very brave and courageous. . . . . Like Me   Not Like Me

III-7 I feel angry when people discriminate against them . . . . Like Me   Not Like Me

III-8 I often ask people to tell me their stories. . . . . Like Me   Not Like Me

III-9 I bond very quickly with most people . . . . Like Me   Not Like Me

III-10 I am good at sensing other people's perspectives . . . . Like Me   Not Like Me

III-11 I often say back to the person what I heard. . . . . Like Me   Not Like Me

III-12 I like to experience the person's world as if I were that person . . . Like Me   Not Like Me

(Go to the Scoring Directions on the next page)

Diversity Communication Scale Scoring

The Diversity Communication Scale is designed to measure your ability to communicate easily with people who are different from you. Teens who are successful in building successful relationships usually value diversity, show effective diversity communication skills, and feel a great deal of empathy when they put themselves in other peoples shoes and think about others' backgrounds and challenges.

These characteristics are prominent and make up the three scales for the assessment.

To score the assessment:

1. Add the number of "Like Me" responses you circled in each of the three previous sections.

2. Then, transfer your totals for each of the three sections to the corresponding lines below.

3. Total all three sections

Section I:	Valuing Diversity Total	= _____
Section II:	Communicating across Cultures Total	= _____
Section III:	Empathy Total	= _____

Three Section TOTAL = _____

Profile Interpretation

Individual Scales Scores	Total Score of All Three Scales	Result	Indications
9 – 12	25 – 36	High	You have the beliefs and behaviors of someone who is comfortable in communications bridging diverse cultures, abilities, characteristics, etc. You are able to work and live effectively with people who are different from you, you are a skilled communicator, and show a great deal of empathy for other people.
4 – 8	13 – 24	Moderate	You have developed some of the beliefs and behaviors of someone who is comfortable in communications bridging diverse cultures, abilities, characteristics, etc You are somewhat able to be with people who are different from you, communicate fairly easily, and you show empathy for other people. You still have some work to do.
0 – 3	0 – 12	Low	You have not yet developed the necessary beliefs and behaviors of someone who is comfortable in communications bridging diverse cultures, abilities, characteristics, etc. You need work on developing skills to get along with people who are different from you. The activities and exercises in this section will help you to develop the skills you need to be an effective communicator in diverse relationships.

For scales which you scored in the **Moderate** or **Low** range, find the descriptions on the pages that follow. Read the description and complete the exercises that are included. No matter how you scored, low, moderate or high, you will benefit from all of these exercises.

Diversity Communication Scale Descriptions

Scale I: Valuing Diversity

Those scoring High on this scale understand the value of enjoying a variety of different people in their world. They value diversity as a resource and enjoy the benefits that diversity brings. They are accepting and welcoming of people different from themselves and get along with people from diverse backgrounds. They are proud of their own background and how they may be different from others and enjoy the pride others show of their own cultures, etc. They work to reduce any prejudices they might have, or that the people around them may have, and tend not to stereotype people different from themselves. They truly believe that all people are to be accepted and respected for who they are.

SCALE II: Communicating Across Cultures

People scoring High on this scale tend to be very good at communicating with people who are different from them. They are aware that others' verbal and non-verbal cues may be different than their own and are aware of how time and space are experienced in different ways. They do not make sweeping generalizations. They are able to notice the similarities, as well as the differences, making them excellent communicators.

SCALE III: Empathy

People scoring High on this scale are easily tuned into other people, whether they are alike or different. They can easily understand what people are feeling, and the intensity of those feelings. When communicating with other people, they bond very quickly. They are attuned to the hidden messages behind what people are saying, and can easily put themselves *into the shoes of others*. They can easily hear between the lines of a normal conversation. They can sense the perspective of others and can experience their world as if they were that person.

People with diversity communication skills are socially skilled and tend to have effective interpersonal relationships. They quickly and easily understand what other people are trying to say, are very intuitive and have developed genuine feelings of compassion and regard for their fellow human beings.

Regardless of your scores on the assessment, you can increase your skills by completing all of the exercises that follow.

Valuing Diversity

Depending on the neighborhood, city, state or country you live in, some locations are more culturally diverse than others. Today, the world is getting smaller because it is becoming more diverse – a good thing! Interacting with people different from you may not come naturally. The process of valuing diversity and learning about people different from you will expand your world. The differences can have a huge range and you will learn something from every single person who is different from you in these ways:

- age
- body/size
- class or social standing
- culture
- emotional sensitivity
- ethnicity

- family
- gender
- mental health
- physical abilities and disabilities
- race

- religion
- sexuality
- spirituality
- talents
- values
- other differences

My Friends

To learn more about the diversity of the people with whom you are friends, complete the following table.

My Friends Who Are Different from Me (name code)	How These Friends are Different from Me
Ex: JBR	Jane was born in Russia, came to this country when she was 10. She only spoke Russian, wore different clothes, and was very shy.

Valuing Diversity – My Diverse Friends

In the table that follows list some of the things you like about your diverse friends.

My Friends Who Are Different from Me (name code)	What I Enjoy About This Person
EX: JBR	*She is so interesting. She speaks another language with her family. Their foods are different than ours and are delicious. They have different customs than we do. She was so shy but now that she has friends, she has become more outgoing and funny!*

© 2013 WHOLE PERSON ASSOCIATES, 210 WEST MICHIGAN ST., DULUTH MN 55802-1908 ▪ 800-247-6789

Valuing Diversity – Who Am I?

It is important that you develop a keen awareness and an appreciation for who YOU are. Complete the following table to better appreciate your own differences.

- age
- body/size
- class or social standing
- culture
- emotional sensitivity
- ethnicity

- family
- gender
- mental health
- physical abilities and disabilities
- race

- religion
- sexuality
- spirituality
- talents
- values
- other differences

Your Differences	How Has this Difference Affected You?
Ex: Size. I am very short.	*People make fun of me because I am so short and not good at most sports but I run fast. I am practicing a lot and now I am on the track team!*

Valuing Diversity – Avoid Stereotyping

The challenge for most people is that because there are such differences in people in the world, miscommunication is likely to happen, especially when there are significant cultural differences between the people talking. Miscommunication often leads to hurt feelings, conflict, or aggravates conflict that already exists.

Stereotypes are over-generalizations, negative or positive ideas about a person or people of any certain group.

These are some negative stereotypes of teens:

- Bad boy
- Bad girl
- Bookworm
- Boy next door
- Bully
- Druggy
- Gangster
- Geek

- Girl next door
- Goth
- Hunk
- Irresponsible
- Jock
- Know-it-all
- Lazy
- Nerd

- Pageant Queens
- Party animal
- Princess
- Punk
- Rebellious
- Rich kids
- Spoiled
- Tomboy

Name some positive things that you would like people to say when talking about teens.

- _____
- _____
- _____
- _____
- _____
- _____
- _____
- _____

- _____
- _____
- _____
- _____
- _____
- _____
- _____
- _____

- _____
- _____
- _____
- _____
- _____
- _____
- _____
- _____

Valuing Diversity – My Stereotypes

All people have stereotypes about people who are different from them. Think about the different types of stereotypes you hold. Because nobody else will see this exercise, be honest about yourself. In the table that follows, think about your stereotypes, whether positive or negative, about some of the people with whom you typically interact. In the left-hand column are some of the groups that have stereotypes associated with them. In the middle column, identify and list some of your stereotypes associated with the group. In the right column explain how or why your stereotypes are inaccurate. (use name codes)

Groups	Stereotypes	How or Why these Stereotypes Are Inaccurate
Ex: Gender	All men are insensitive	Men in my family are very sensitive and thoughtful
Age		
Body/Size		
Class or Social Standing		
Culture		
Emotional Sensitivity		
Ethnicity		
Family		
Gender		

(Continued on the next page)

Valuing Diversity – My Stereotypes *(Continued)*

Groups	Stereotypes	How or Why these Stereotypes Are Inaccurate
Mental Health		
Physical Abilities and Disabilities		
Race		
Religion		
Sexuality		
Spirituality		
Talents		
Values		
Other Differences		
Other Differences		
Other Differences		

Valuing Diversity – Communicating with Someone Different from Me

The best way to connect with people that are different from you is to get to know them. The more you are able to interact with people different from you, the less you will stereotype and the better you will be at getting along with everyone. Identify someone who is different from you in some way and have a discussion with this person about anything. After your conversation, complete the questions that follow to explore your ability to be open and non-judgmental.

The person I communicated with _____(use name code)

The stereotype(s) I have heard about this type of person are _____
_____
_____

This person is different from me in the following way(s): _____
_____
_____

This person is the same as me in the following way(s): _____
_____
_____

I respect this person because _____
_____
_____

I communicated by _____
_____
_____

The other person communicated by_____
_____
_____

My body language_____
_____
_____

The other person's body language _____
_____
_____

(Continued on the next page)

Communicating with Someone Different from Me

MY REACTIONS

Did you listen actively? _____ How did you show this? _____

_____

_____

_____

In what ways were you able to put yourself in the other person's shoes? _____

_____

_____

_____

What did that experience feel like? _____

_____

_____

_____

Did either of you mention anything about your differences? _____

_____

_____

_____

Did you like this person? _____ Why or why not? _____

_____

_____

_____

What did you learn from this exercise? _____

_____

_____

_____

Empathy

Empathy is at the very heart of all conversations you have with other people. Empathic listening, however, is not as easy as it sounds. Empathic listening involves putting yourself in someone else's shoes and trying to understand his or her position.

Preparation for Empathic Listening

Think about a conversation you recently had with someone culturally different from you. Who was the person and what were you talking about? (use name code)

Person:_____

Topic of Conversation:_____

_____

_____

_____

_____

Answer the following questions related to your conversation:

How did you pay attention, both physically and emotionally, and listen to the person's point of view? What was the result?

_____

_____

_____

_____

How did you try to set your judgments and biases aside for the moment and walk in the shoes of the person? How did that work for you?

_____

_____

_____

_____

(Continued on the next page)

Empathy *(Continued)*

As the person spoke, how did you listen especially for the messages behind the words? What did you hear?

_____

_____

_____

_____

_____

How were messages being sent by the person non-verbally through body language? What messages did you receive?

_____

_____

_____

_____

_____

How frequently but briefly did you respond to the person's actual messages? How did that affect your conversation?

_____

_____

_____

_____

_____

After you responded with empathy, what cues did you receive that either confirm or deny the accuracy of your response? What was that experience like for you? What was the experience like for the other person?

_____

_____

_____

_____

_____

Diversity Quotations

Read each quotation and write your interpretation and how it relates to you.

I know there is strength in the differences between us.
I know there is comfort, where we overlap.
~ Ani DiFranco

_____

_____

_____

_____

Different roads sometimes lead to the same castle.
~ George R.R. Martin

_____

_____

_____

_____

What we have to do . . . is to find a way to celebrate our diversity
and debate our differences without fracturing our communities.
~ Hilary Clinton

_____

_____

_____

_____

Controversial as we all know, is often a euphemism
for interesting and intelligent.
~ Kevin Smith

_____

_____

_____

_____

The Ineffective Diversity Communication Cycle

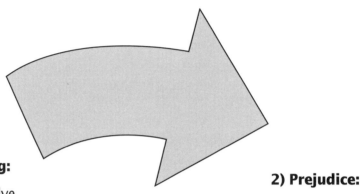

1) Stereotyping:

Stereotypes involve generalizations about the "typical" characteristics of members of the groups.

2) Prejudice:

An attitude toward the members of some group based solely on their membership in that group (can be positive or negative).

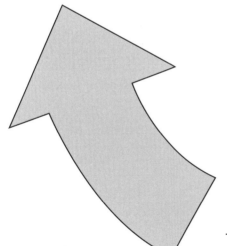

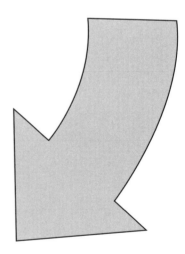

3) Discrimination:

The actual positive or negative actions toward the objects of prejudice.

Effective Diversity Communication

Following are some ways to work on your communication skills:

- Be aware of the possibility of differences. Never assume that other people are like you. Be open and flexible in your communication with others.

- Acknowledge and respect the differences in all people.

- Don't assume that your way is the right way to communicate. Keep questioning your assumptions about the right way to communicate. Research diversity communication on the Internet. How do different cultures communicate in ways different than you?

- Watch your body language. Postures that indicate friendliness in one culture might indicate aggressiveness in another. Research non-verbal communication differences in cultures. How do various cultures communicate differently through body language?

- Listen actively and empathetically. Try to put yourself in the other person's shoes. Especially when another person's perceptions or ideas are very different from your own, you might need to operate at the edge of your own comfort zone. How can you begin listening more actively?

- If someone speaks a different language, or is hearing impaired, speak clearly, at a normal pace and a normal volume. Maintain good eye contact.

- Be patient. People who speak your language as a second language may have to translate what you've said into their home language then try to convert their response back into yours.

- Provide instructions in a clear sequence. Never assume that the other person knows what you are talking about or has done the task before. Write instructions down if necessary.

- Check for understanding – ask questions which require more than a yes or no answer.

SECTION V:

Negotiation Style Scale

Name_____

Date_____

Negotiation Style Scale
Directions

Disagreements are a natural part of any relationship. Negotiation is a special skill from which everyone benefits. Your ability to negotiate will allow you to get what you want without alienating or manipulating others and reach a mutually agreeable solution. This often involves compromise.

The Negotiation Style Scale is designed to help you understand more about the type of negotiator that you are, and it will provide you with insights into the negotiation styles of people with whom you have relationships.

This booklet contains 28 statements that are divided into four negotiation process styles. Read each statement and decide the extent to which the statement describes you.

Circle 3 if the statement is **A Lot Like Me**

Circle 2 if the statement is **A Little Like Me**

Circle 1 if the statement is **Not Like Me**

In the negotiating process with another person,

I-1 – I prefer to discuss the problem. 3   (2)   1

In the above statement, the circled 2 means that the statement is a little like the participant. Ignore the TOTAL lines below each section. They are for scoring purposes and will be used later.

This is not a test and there are no right or wrong answers. Do not spend too much time thinking about your answers. Your initial response will likely be the most true for you. Be sure to respond to every statement.

(Turn to the next page and begin)

Negotiation Style Scale

3 = A Lot Like Me　　**2 = A Little Like Me**　　**1 = Not Like Me**

In the negotiating process with another person,

I-1	I prefer to discuss the problem	3	2	1
I-2	I can be very convincing	3	2	1
I-3	I like to talk more than I like to listen.	3	2	1
I-4	I become very emotional	3	2	1
I-5	I like to rely on gut feelings rather than logic	3	2	1
I-6	I skip from topic to topic often	3	2	1
I-7	I get bored quickly with too many details	3	2	1

I - TOTAL = _____

3 = A Lot Like Me　　**2 = A Little Like Me**　　**1 = Not Like Me**

In the negotiating process with another person,

II-1	I like to have more facts than I really need	3	2	1
II-2	I am assertive	3	2	1
II-3	I have clear goals about what I want	3	2	1
II-4	I like to have every detail at my fingertips.	3	2	1
II-5	I stay extremely focused	3	2	1
II-6	I am determined to talk about details	3	2	1
II-7	I see negotiation as a game to win	3	2	1

II - TOTAL = _____

(Continued on the next page)

Negotiation Style Scale *(Continued)*

3 = A Lot Like Me   2 = A Little Like Me   1 = Not Like Me

In the negotiating process with another person,

III-1 I can be overwhelming with my preparations 3   2   1

III-2 I like to get to the end result as quickly as possible 3   2   1

III-3 I believe that being prepared is the key. 3   2   1

III-4 I am able to defend my beliefs. 3   2   1

III-5 I like to show proof that I know what I am talking about. 3   2   1

III-6 I stay right on track 3   2   1

III-7 I am able to clearly back up my beliefs 3   2   1

III - TOTAL = _____

3 = A Lot Like Me   2 = A Little Like Me   1 = Not Like Me

In the negotiating process with another person,

IV-1 I am guided by my emotions when I am listening to
someone else's views 3   2   1

IV-2 I ask others for assistance and listen to what they say 3   2   1

IV-3 I am a very good listener 3   2   1

IV-4 I do not like to be the only one talking 3   2   1

IV-5 I am interested in hearing the smallest of details 3   2   1

IV-6 I negotiate based on my values and stay open to understanding
of the other person's values 3   2   1

IV-7 I understand that I may need to compromise 3   2   1

IV - TOTAL = _____

(Go to the Scoring Directions on the next page)

Negotiation Style Scale
Scoring Directions

The Negotiating Style Scale is designed to identify the style you use when you are negotiating with other people.

Transfer your totals for each of the four sections to the lines below:

SECTION I	**TALKER**	**TOTAL** =	_____
SECTION II	**STEAM-ROLLER**	**TOTAL** =	_____
SECTION III	**PREPARER**	**TOTAL** =	_____
SECTION IV	**LISTENER**	**TOTAL** =	_____

Profile Interpretation

Total Individual Scales Scores	Result	Indications
17 to 21	High	In the negotiation process, you tend to use many of the characteristics of this negotiation process style.
12 to 16	Moderate	In the negotiation process, you tend to use some of the characteristics of this negotiation process style.
7 to 11	Low	In the negotiation process, you tend to use very few of the characteristics of this negotiation process style.

Conflict happens when two people have different opinions about an issue or issues and cannot resolve it easily or calmly. There is no one best style to use in all situations when you are negotiating. Each of the styles can be useful in different situations. People do not have one specific style for negotiating; they are able to use all four styles. Many of us, however, rely on and get comfortable using one of the styles more often than the others.

The area in which you scored the highest tends to be the negotiation style you use most. Similarly, the area in which you scored the lowest tends to be your least used negotiation style. To learn more about why you prefer one style more than the others, turn to the next page for a description of each of the four styles on the assessment. Please answer the questions related to each of the styles.

Negotiation Style Scale
Profile Descriptions

SCALE I — TALKER: People with a Talker Negotiation Style prefer to talk through the negotiation process and to lead the pace of the process. They prefer to talk rather than listen, and they rely on their conversational skills to try to guide the negotiating process. They tend to rely more on emotions and gut feelings than on logic and analysis. In the end, they need to feel good about the end results.

List times when this negotiating style has worked well for you. (use name codes)

_____

_____

_____

_____

_____

_____

List times when this negotiating style has not worked well for you. (use name codes)

_____

_____

_____

_____

_____

_____

What patterns do you notice? (use name codes)

_____

_____

_____

_____

_____

_____

(Continued on the next page)

Negotiation Style Scale
Profile Descriptions *(Continued)*

SCALE II — STEAM-ROLLER: People with a Steam Roller Negotiating Style rely on facts and logic to accomplish their purpose and meet their needs. They have clear goals and tend to try to overpower others with little regard to emotions. They can become aggressive if pushed in the negotiation process. They are primarily concerned about succeeding in getting what they want out of the negotiation process. They like to be in control of the process and will do what they need to do in order to win.

List times when this negotiation style has worked well for you. (use name codes)

_____

_____

_____

_____

_____

_____

List times when this negotiation style has not worked well for you. (use name codes)

_____

_____

_____

_____

_____

_____

What patterns do you notice? (use name codes)

_____

_____

_____

_____

_____

_____

(Continued on the next page)

Negotiation Style Scale
Profile Descriptions *(Continued)*

SCALE III — PREPARER: People with a Preparer Negotiation Process Style believe that proof of what is right will often determine the outcome of the negotiation. They believe that if you cannot prove your point, then why even negotiate. They have little need for emotions and feel that emotions play no part in the negotiation process. They like to be prepared and believe that the best prepared people win in the negotiation process.

List times when this negotiation style has worked well for you. (use name codes)

_____

_____

_____

_____

_____

_____

List times when this negotiation style has not worked well for you. (use name codes)

_____

_____

_____

_____

_____

_____

What patterns do you notice? (use name codes)

_____

_____

_____

_____

_____

_____

(Continued on the next page)

Negotiation Style Scale
Profile Descriptions *(Continued)*

SCALE IV — LISTENER: People with a Listener Negotiation Process Style usually prefer listening to talking or arguing. They will gladly accept assistance from other people during the process because they do not enjoy participating in the negotiation process. They are guided by their value system, and the process is often more important to them than the end results. They respect the rules of the negotiating process and desire win-win end results.

List times when this negotiation style has worked well for you. (use name codes)

_____

_____

_____

_____

_____

_____

List times when this negotiation style has not worked well for you. (use name codes)

_____

_____

_____

_____

_____

_____

What patterns do you notice? (use name codes)

_____

_____

_____

_____

_____

_____

Negotiation Situations

It is important to identify and understand the situations which require you to negotiate. The next two exercises will help you learn more about where and with whom you negotiate.

Where My Negotiations Occur

List where and with whom most of your negotiations occur. (use name codes)

Where They Occur	With Whom They Occur
Ex: In my home	MAF

When My Negotiations Occur

List when most of your negotiations occur and what you dislike about the situation that causes you to feel uncomfortable.

When They Occur	What I Dislike about the Situation
Ex: When my friends come over.	MAF becomes aggressive and I am embarrassed.

Negotiation Process Worksheet

Identify a major negotiation that you have been involved in during the past year. This could have been with a member of your family, friend, peer, girlfriend, boyfriend, neighbor, co-worker, boss or teacher. (use name codes)

Negotiation Situation: _____

_____

_____

_____

1. What strategy or negotiation process style(s) did you use?

_____

_____

_____

2. What strategy or negotiation process(es) did the other person use?

_____

_____

_____

3. What did you want? What did the other person want?

_____

_____

_____

4. What was the result of the negotiation?

_____

_____

_____

5. What strategies did you use to bring the resolution to a conclusion?

_____

_____

_____

Negotiation Patterns

List five different times you have negotiated. What strategies did you use and how effective were the results?

What Was the Issue?	My Strategies	What Were the Results?
Ex: My parents wanted me to go to an out-of-state university. I'd like to go to a local community college.	I downloaded info about the costs of five universities and the grades I would need to have.	I was able to convince them that a community college was the best place for me to further my education.

Ideal Negotiations

Write about a current situation in which you find yourself in a conflict or disagreement and will need to negotiate.

1) Conflict and disagreement are inevitable.

List a negotiation situation that you are facing:

_____

_____

_____

_____

2) Getting angry and frustrated will not help.

How can you avoid getting upset and angry in the situation?

_____

_____

_____

_____

3) Consider individual people or groups that will be affected in the situation.

Who are the individual people or groups who will be affected by your negotiation? (use name codes)

_____

_____

_____

_____

4) Separate feelings from the negotiation process.

How can you do this?

_____

_____

_____

_____

(Continued on the next page)

Ideal Negotiations *(Continued)*

5) Focus on outcomes, not positions.

What are your desired outcomes of this negotiation?

_____

_____

_____

_____

6) Identify mutually agreeable solutions.

What is the solution you would like?

_____

_____

_____

_____

7) Be flexible.

How can you remain flexible during the negotiation process?

_____

_____

_____

_____

8) Come to an agreement.

How can you and the other party come to some sort of agreement?

_____

_____

_____

_____

Negotiation Quotation

> *The most important trip you may take in life*
> *is meeting people half way.*
>
> **~ Henry Boyle**

What does this quote mean to you?

_____

_____

_____

_____

_____

When do you think it is appropriate?

_____

_____

_____

_____

_____

When do you think it is not appropriate?

_____

_____

_____

_____

_____

If you could, how would you reword it to make it fit your life better?

_____

_____

_____

_____

_____

Being a Better Negotiator

Write about what you can start doing today to become a better negotiator.

_____
_____
_____
_____
_____
_____
_____
_____
_____
_____
_____

Learned Attributes of Negotiations

Describe some of the attributes of the other negotiation types that you would like to possess and why.

_____
_____
_____
_____
_____
_____
_____
_____
_____
_____
_____
_____

Principles of Successful Negotiation

- Understanding that conflict and disagreement are inevitable.

- Getting angry and frustrated will not help.

- The other person has a different interest or agenda.

- The other person's position may also be valuable.

- Separate your own feelings from the process of negotiating.

- Focus on outcomes, not your initial viewpoint.

- Identify positions on which you both agree.

- Be flexible and willing to compromise.

- Come to an agreement.

- Negotiating and debating are not the same.

Debating vs. Negotiating

There is often some confusion about the differences between debating and negotiating. Although they can appear to be the same, debating and negotiating are very different in nature. The following table outlines the differences between these two forms of communicating.

DEBATING	NEGOTIATION
Encourages arguments	Encourages a win-win mutually agreed upon solution
Has strict rules of conduct to observe	Is spontaneous in nature
Often a team event	Often occurs between individuals
Agreed upon in advance	Can occur at any time
People attempt to refute the other's position	People compromise to find a solution

Four Negotiations Styles

SCALE I — TALKER

People with a Talker Negotiation-Process Style prefer to talk through the negotiation process and to dictate the pace of the process. They prefer to talk rather than listen, and they rely on their conversational skills to try to control the negotiating process. How do you think most people react to this style?

SCALE II — STEAM-ROLLER

People with a Steam-roller Negotiating Style rely on facts and logic to accomplish their purpose and meet their needs. They have clear goals and tend to try to overpower others with little regard to emotions. How do you think most people react to this style?

SCALE III — PREPARER

People with a Preparer Negotiation-Process Style believe that proof of what is right will often determine the outcome of the negotiation. They believe that if you cannot prove your point logically, then why even negotiate. How do you think most people react to this style?

SCALE IV — LISTENER

People with a Listener Negotiation-Process Style usually prefer listening to talking or arguing. They will gladly accept assistance from other people during the process because they do not enjoy the negotiation process. How do you think most people react to this style?

wholeperson

Whole Person Associates is the leading publisher
of training resources for professionals who empower

people to create and maintain healthy lifestyles.
Our creative resources will help you work effectively with

your clients in the areas of stress management,
wellness promotion, mental health and life skills.

Please visit us at our web site: **www.wholeperson.com**.
You can check out our entire line of products,
place an order, request our print catalog, and
sign up for our monthly special notifications.

Whole Person Associates

210 W Michigan

Duluth MN 55802

800-247-6789